SING ME DOWN FROM THE DARK

ALEXANDRA CORRIN-TACHIBANA

Sing Me Down from the Dark

SALT

CROMER

PUBLISHED BY SALT PUBLISHING 2022

2 4 6 8 10 9 7 5 3 1

First published in Great Britain in 2022 by
Salt Publishing Ltd
12 Norwich Road, Cromer, Norfolk NR27 0AX United Kingdom

www.saltpublishing.com

Salt Publishing Limited Reg. No. 5293401

A CIP catalogue record for this book is available from the British Library

ISBN 978 1 78463 276 2 (Paperback edition)

Typeset in Sabon by Salt Publishing

Printed and bound in Great Britain by Clays Ltd, Elcograf S.p.A

To G.

Contents

*

*

*

SING ME DOWN FROM THE DARK

Coming Home

My sister tells me I needn't speak slowly
and make exaggerated movements.
I wait for the Sainsbury's cashier
to pack my bags like in *Fujiya*,
for taxi doors to open for me.
I miss the driver's white gloves.
The trains are grubby and I crave
cold *Asahi Super Dry* from the trolley
with the pink-suited bowing lady
and the eel *obento* boxes.
The *sushi* sucks and I can only find
California rolls, salmon or tuna,
but not my favourite, oily *engawa*:
the tail fin muscle of a flatfish.
I miss *miso* soup for a hangover
and I miss the word for a hangover:
futsukayoi (second day drunkenness).
I miss what I once heard as jibberish,
on the phone a high-pitched
moshi moshi: Hello; ladies giggling
at men, with their hands over mouths;
and all the other at first annoying things,
right down to the smell
of the fading *tatami*.

Single Mum, in a Japanese Office, near St. Paul's

I run to the nursery gate, fall flat on my face, and stop
at The Co-op on our way home, to buy two bottles
of Red. *This bus is for Ruislip*, you mimic. And the
passengers smile. Later, you cut a chunk out of your
fringe, and your father rings from Japan: it will be
3 years until he can save enough to live with us. I
wonder if I can wait that long. I take you to the Natural
History Museum to see Diplodocus. I tell my friend
how I was not invited to the *Bonenkai* (忘年会),
'Forget the Year' party. How instead, the cleaners and
security guards took me for a Brick Lane curry. How I
carried the company Christmas Tree from the Service
Lift across the 33rd floor balcony. How decorating
it was the best bit of my job. How I paid special
attention to glittery, low-hanging baubles, guarding
them carefully, from smashing open, on the office floor.

At the Fishmonger's with my Son

His eyes glisten.
The Lindsey brother sees us, heads
to the fridge for the *sashimi* salmon.

Far from Suruga Bay, my son knows little of Japan
except for Pokémon, and when he grows up
he's going to buy a *sashimi* farm.

He knows nothing of bowing.
Nothing of the uncle who wouldn't hold him.
Nothing of his aunt, Suzuko.

Nothing of a wooden house,
a quilted stove,
peeling winter tangerines.

My son's eyes glisten,
like the *sashimi* salmon
he begs the Lindsey brother to cut more of.

写真
Photos

I picture you emerging like a Labrador from Tenryu river,
wetsuited and grinning through soaked black hair.
And I don't forget how we laughed on Cebu Island,
when the room key broke in the lock. Our faces,
when they handed us a Welcome Mango
on the bus. How we watched kids weeing
into shanty streets, wondering where on earth
we were going. And the waiter, serenading me
on his ukulele: *Darling You Look Wonderful Tonight*. Sleeping deeply
on the 成田エクスプレス to my second home. Bare calves strewn
across your lap. Engaged, on the hot spring Izu Peninsula.
How we bathed in our nothingness. *Skinship*, the Japanese call it.
Yes, I recall how we really did exist beyond photos buried
in the wardrobe. Yes, my stranger husband. Once, we were a fit.

成田エクスプレス: Narita Express

[4]

*

A Personal Glossary

daikon: a phallic white radish diced for soup
some grow to small human size

enka: a sentimental *karaoke* song
and form of seduction

gamman: endurance
of the workplace, losing face, cheating partners

irasshai: welcome to my home
but stack shoes in the rack

kobe niku: marbled beef
from cows fed beer and massaged

netsuke: sensual, delicate carvings
adorning *samurai* swords

sumimasen: sorry, thank you, excuse me
repeated insincerely

yochien: nursery, where Japanese babies can tell
if other babies do not know this word

Sensei

I.

The Japanese
could make hammocks
out of my bras,
Irish Tara laughs
through red-wine teeth.
We plan how to spend 22 grand,
learn greetings,
pack Heinz Baked Beans
and head for Narita.

II.

On the balcony,
Yutaka shows me
the washing machine.
Futons are in a musty cupboard,
air con above the bed, a fan
by the phone. It clicks as it rotates.
Yutaka leaves, and I stare
at my size 8 feet,
on square-matted *tatami*.

III.

Kangai-kai welcome party:
jugs of *Asahi*,
sparrow on sticks,
the Shizuoka speciality, dolphin,
and a well-equipped
Snack Bar toilet,
with a bidet button
and musical fanfare
while you pee.

IV.

Sweat, in the small of my back.
They say a foreigner
smells of butter,
has different ear-wax;
guess my blood-type
for hints about my personality;
tell me dairy makes me *kakkoii* –
tall, with *sharp* features.
Alien Registration cards
must be carried
at all times.

Japanese Bathing Etiquette

I sit on pink plastic the size of a potty, scrub my entire body. The naked Japanese women sit beside me in rows. Breasts and bottoms. 'Mongolian spots', like little bruises on their bum-cheeks. We move from boiling springs to freezing springs to open-air. Yumi, a hostess, goes daily to sweat out the alcohol. But nothing beats a *Kirin* beer in your *yukata* gown after a bath. Only tonight is different.

Two *obasan* stand on the side of the *sento* trying to break me. *Dete kudasai! Dete kudasai!* I sit in a steaming pool. I don't want to leave. 'I don't understand,' I say, in English. I am the only *gaijin*. The white-uniformed women wait it out until I emerge to grab my modesty towel. I've broken bathing rules posted in the changing room lockers, because of the tiny snake tattoo, on my left buttock.

Gaijin: foreigner, 'outside person'

Love-love desu ne!

Yoshiteru, your name, like
ashiteru – I love you

you sang it to me at *karaoke* –
sweet as *sukiyaki* beef.

You loved my bob,
my boobs, my waist,

my heart-shaped face.
I loved your black hair,

your Harley, your rock star
sunglasses; the first sunrise of 1998

on Miho beach.
You loved to speak English.

For two months,
I'd answer the phone

in my best *moshi moshi* – Hello!
You'd say, *Hello Darling. I am Teru.*

Love-love desu ne: 'loved up'

Portrait of a Gaijin

I have brown eyes but some of you
have rendered them blue
and made me a blonde.

I am not 'black-eyed' like you.
You oil-paint me for the citizens'
public hall project, *Foreigners*.

I am *gaijin* of the week, English,
my portrait to be displayed
in Shizuoka City Library.

I understand your terms.
I hear *shibo* and *kiniku*.
Is that fat or muscle on her arms?

Bride Face

I wore a wooden wig,
heavy gold *kimono*,
geisha-face and *geta*.
I recited words.

They loved my foreign
bride face, my brown bob.
They loved our
kokusai kekkon.
They loved me
in ivory and tiara,
singing *karaoke*.

Our honeymoon
I have tried to forget.

Have tried to forget
your persistence,
your summoning
of Sorrento waiters
with a *sumimasen*.

Have not forgotten
how you wanted
to go home early.
Missed food, missed work,
missed your mother
tongue. You were a
chonan, first son,
with filial
obligation.

Happy Happy Happy!

I'm singing Titanic
arms stretched out

barefoot
at the *karaoke* box

swaying side to side
bellowing into a gold mic.

Hiroyuki Morimae is behind me
arms around my waist

mouth gaping open
laughing.

Pink felt hearts frame the shot
with words cut

from rich *origami* paper
stuck in a scrapbook:

Happy Happy Happy!

Like the little messages
pink and white

on fizzy *Love Hearts* sweets
children love to share and read.

Picture of Haru

It was the day you bought me sweet potato from a street stall –
our helmeted heads, together, in Ray-Bans, in the photo
that made my sister laugh so hard she got it framed.
When we split, your mother cried and your father apologised;
he was sorry that his son wasn't good enough.

East is East and West is West my dad said at the start, but soon
they got used to you opening the car door for Mum, trying to be
an English gentleman, your creased eyes and cracked feet,
your mother's hands and your father's face, and you, Haru,
chasing me with the pig's trotters for the noodle broth.

本栖湖

Lake Motosuko, September 2003

You dressed for the occasion
albeit in double denim
but that was you, born in 1960

my 43-year-old Japanese Travolta
with *Night Fever* moves
and me on your arm.

Walking around Motosuko
we stopped circling the issues:
you were a *chonan*, eldest son

I wanted a future in Britain –
impossible! We'd talked
of a *Sushi-ya san* in London

you, a fishmonger's son
could slice the oily underbelly
from a Hokkaido salmon.

Staring into the deepest
of the Five Lakes
of Fuji-san, we ended.

Heart of a Japanese

Your dad called me *Musume* – daughter.
He liked to take me out to dinner.
He had fish killed from the tank for my *sashimi*.
Your mum made me sushi at home.
It pleased them to watch me eat:

kokoro ga nipponjin desu ne –
you have the heart of a Japanese.

In a family diner, I concentrate on my curry rice.
Tomorrow we'll go to City Hall on your bike,
to divorce. Your mum dribbles. You wipe her.
Soothe her with jokes. I watch her stroke-ravaged
face crumple, to cry, into her *donburi* rice bowl.

10 Years; 10 Places

Hamamatsu: home of *unagi pie* – a biscuit made of eel.

Iwakuni: bridge of *samurai* – beer with strangers under blossom.

Burracho's bar: grilled sparrow on a stick and flirtation with the 'Master'.

Nara: home of mountain deer, warm porridge-like rice wine – *amazake*.

Miyajima: an island, Hiroshima oysters. More deer.

Yumigahama: a bow-shaped beach, barbecued mackerel, got engaged.

Kyoto: by taxi to Kinkakuji; driver, in white gloves, holding an umbrella
for my mother.

Fukuoka: *fu*, not fuck. *Karaoke* till 5 a.m. and hangovers in a hot spring.

Ryukyu: home of *Awamori* – an Okinawan brew with a snake in.

Shizuoka: still hill, located on a fault line.

*

Kotoshi mo yoroshiku
Thank you for your support for this year in advance

一月 *ichi-gatsu*: New Year family party and mother-in-law's watching me eat slippery fatty tuna with chopsticks. Our feet are beside a *kotatsu* stove and I'm having to shift positions, alternating between cross-legged, kneeling, and stretching out onto *tatami*. 二月 *ni-gatsu*: Shinobu takes me on his bike to Bow Beach. We stop to pet a Pomeranian, belonging to a wanna-be-American on his Harley. They pose in matching bomber jackets. The dog, in sunglasses. 三月 *san-gatsu* is *Hinamatsuri* month: Girls' Day. Mother-in-law puts tiered ornamental dolls on display. 四月 *shi-gatsu* is for cherry blossom viewing. I drink Anglo-Japanese Society beer, *kampai* with strangers, listen to praise for our Viking noses. 五月 *go-gatsu* is *shirasu* season – baby white sardines piled high on rice. Black dot for an eye. 六月 *roku-gatsu*: *jime jime* sweat on my skin. A stranger runs after me. Gives me her umbrella, in the June rain. 七月 *shichi-gatsu*: wet heat. My rotating fan hums. I spot a *gokiburi* above my futon. Get up. Hoover it off the ceiling. 'Song' of cicada persists. 八月 *hachi-gatsu*: stepping out at Heathrow I see Brits through non-British eyes. How overweight they are. How greasy their Fish n Chips. 九月 *ku-gatsu* marks the start of school. Students chant *onegaishimasu*! Bow at beginning and end of class. And then there's earthquake drill! 十月 *juu-gatsu* is the Shimizu Kokusai Open Day. Yutaka Sensei's on guitar. I sing, 'Hey Jude.' 十一月 *juuichi-gatsu* provides respite. A trip to Nico to see 'The Changing of the Leaves' and hot spring monkeys. 十二月 *juuni-gatsu*: finally, it's *Bonenkai*.

'Goodbye to the Year' party. Fishy egg custard. 'Are you strong for alcohol?' 'Can you eat *umeboshi* sour plum?'And Unno Sensei's speech. In English. Struggling to differentiate between *l* and *r* sounds, he asks all the teachers to 'do a big crap'.

Jime jime: the feeling of humidity

Gokiburi: cockroach

The Road to Ippon Matsu

We biked through the seasons:
Spring, *sakura* blossom,

Summer, sardines by the river,
Autumn, volcanic eggs by Hakone Lake,

Winter, snow on Bow Beach.
Our twenty-something selves,

you a black-lashed boy,
me, *aka no tanin* – a red stranger.

Steeped in tea terraces, we rode
to Ippon Matsu Shrine and made a pledge.

Wakeboarding, in Hamamatsu

You zip me
    into a pink and white wetsuit
                    squashing my boobs:
        it belonged to Saiichi's ex
                    half-American and 173 centimetres tall
            you cup my head
                        it's smaller
                            than a Japanese
                                how young I look
                                    in my summer cap
                                you attach me
        to a board   pull me by a cord
            behind your jet-ski
                I weigh more than the 45 kilos of a
    Japanese lady
struggle to balance
                your friends applaud
                    as I plummet
                            into the Tenryu river
                                how *lucky* they found me a wetsuit!
                    we drink Asahi
                    eat mackerel
            round a disposable barbecue
        Sister-in-law
    Machiko
        tells a story
                about your ex   her friend
                                a high school teacher
                    who she says was *kawaii* – pretty
        she knows I understand

          cleaning up after lunch
      is a group activity
                but there are too many hands
                        I'm left to observe
                                bowing
                                thanking each other
                                for taking care of one another
                        people are hesitant
                to leave first
          bow again say *sumimasen* – Thank You Sorry Apologies
even though we're in Crocs and shorts
                        have peed in the estuary
                                and peeled off sodden wetsuits
                        so awkwardly
            behind car doors

Red Strangers

You walked up to me and asked if you could practice
English. Said, in Japanese, you'd worked overseas, surfed
the Australian Gold Coast, were 36 years old and an
'International Businessman' of Takahashi Corporation.
Bowing, you presented me *meishi*. I said, 'if you want to
practice English, why don't you speak in English'? We
were *aka-no-tanin*: red strangers. You, from Shizuoka-Shi,
the 'quiet hill', famed for green tea and *sashimi*. Me, from
Bradford-on-Avon, the 'broad river crossing', with a Saxon
Church and Wiltshire ham. Walking away, I turned and
watched you wave. You, in your navy-blue 'salaryman' suit.

Meishi: business cards

Bow Beach

Your slim brown hands
which don't yet wear a wedding band
use chopsticks
to turn the mackerel
in its criss-crossed silver coat
studded with sea salt.

The oily white flesh
tastes like kipper
only different.
This is *Yumigahama*
and we're here to show Sally
the best of Japan.

She and I swim
then listen to you talk
about our little foreign faces
bobbing on the waves.
Sally's like a Fifties movie star, you say,
her blue eyes and boyish hair.

I don't yet know
that our child will be a boy,
that we'll call him *Ryoma* –
Dragon Horse,
and that I'll be holding
his slim brown hands.

ダーリンは外国人
'My Darling is a Foreigner'

She steps out onto our balcony in bare feet
our toddler follows her as she hangs laundry
She does not wear straw slippers
she does not rinse sticky rice before cooking

Our toddler follows her as she hangs laundry
she won't let *Okasan* give him sugar cubes for hiccups
she does not rinse sticky rice before cooking
my darling is a foreigner

She won't let *Okasan* give our son sugar cubes for hiccups
she does not soak her heels before bed
my darling is a *gaijin*
She does not peel the skin of a Fuji apple

she does not soak her heels before bed
she does not eat fruit bits with toothpicks
She does not peel the skin of a Fuji apple
or enter *Okasan's* kitchen

My darling is an outside person
she does not wear straw slippers
she does not drink *matcha* tea
She steps out onto our balcony in bare feet

Miyajima, with Sally

At the floating red *torii*,
performing the peace sign,
with a bunch of giggly girls
wearing knee-highs.
On the shore, Itsukushima Shrine
stable, red and white,
like the *Hinomaru* flag;
a white, life-sized wooden horse greets us.
The real thing used to be sacrificed for the gods.
Lines of white paper bows
hanging in rows, a laundry rack of wishes:
good grades, riches, fertility.
I link arms with a wooden *Fukuroji*,
God of longevity, as tall as me:
bald, bearded, holding a staff;
chuckling inside his phallic head.
Sally takes another photo.
We line up behind 'carnival cutouts',
transformed: into cable-car riding monkeys,
a bearded-man in a *yukata* gown with a
fan, and a fireman, holding a gigantic rice
spoon. In and out of stand-ins,
in our white T-shirts and *GAP* jeans –
they think we are twins.
But Sally will take the royal blue striped
shinkansen to Tokyo. To go
home. While I step into my
Japanese life, *gaijin* eyes
peeping out.

Torii: traditional gate to a Shinto shrine

Cross-Cultural Communication in the Homeplace

Tachibana's frown

> when he comes home late
> to find a playpen
> in the *tatami* space

And the disappointment

> at hanging laundry
> on the balcony
> without wearing
> outdoor slippers

And the need to push

> our son's head down
> to teach him
> to bow
> before he can talk

Farewell to カラオケ

I don't eat giant Miho strawberries,
or Fuji apples dressed
in polystyrene doilies, like tutus.
And I don't spot *tanuki* fox dogs
at dusk, as I leave work.
I don't buy sour plum rice triangles,
folded in seaweed, from the *konbini*.
Or float in hot springs at *ryokan* inns,
eat baby sardines, in the Shizuokan summer.
I don't boil *onsen* eggs in volcanic lakes.
Or ski Nagano's slopes with *Otosan*.
Nor do I sleep in the passenger seat
beside my husband-to-be,
until we reach the resort. I don't duet
Endless Love with *Snack Bar* host,
Kazuma, for strangers sipping *Oolong-Hai*.
And I don't have a bottle of *shōchū*
on the 'drinking shop' shelf, my name tag,
in *katakana*. I don't ride on Harleys
to Love Hotels. Or, barefoot in a box,
learn Okinawan song, 涙そうそう,
pretending to be Natsugawa Rimi.
And I don't sing: *Great Tears Are Spilling;*
at the top of my *gaijin* voice.

カラオケ: *katakana* script for *karaoke*

Konbini: *konbiniensu sutoru*, 'convenience store'

涙そうそう: read as *nada sou sou*

Ghazal for my husband, on International Women's Day

The box of Thorntons from Asda feels consumerist and cliché.
I'm never going to leave this house. Enjoy the chocolates darling, you say.

How's your hobby going? you ask, close up and in my way.
We never had problems until this poetry thing. Am I annoying darling? you say.

You bellow *Good Morning*, ask how I slept, and then, your daily refrain,
shot up the driveway like a golf ball: *have a nice day darling*, you say.

I'm chasing you and you're chasing our son. Like a triangle, you claim.
Omoshiroi ne, you laugh, and draw him away. *Funny isn't it, darling?* you say.

You photograph an empty wine bottle, a sink in disarray.
I ask why on earth you'd do such a thing: *I don't remember darling*, you say.

You take my work-from-home computer. *You don't appreciate me*, you complain.
But later there's reframing: *I was making it more efficient darling*, you say.

Alex-chan, watashi no okusan, thank you for letting me stay.
I start, on hearing my Japanese pet name. *I love you, darling*, you say.

Watashi no okusan: my wife

[31]

マスク
Masks

Upstairs / from the spare room / your voice booms
on Zoom. / Clipped / set phrases / of the workplace. /
Downstairs / I eat a bacon sandwich. / Our countries have
a 9-hour difference. / But we've been in the same zone /
for 16 weeks. / You eat separately. / In your own time. /
Won't eat my roast chicken. / In Nippon / it was sliced.
/ Deep-fried *karaage* / *yakitori* bites / *tebasaki* wings. / I
could only buy the whole thing / at Christmas. / Would
cook it in a Toaster Oven. / I watch you add Golden
Curry spice bricks / to my Jamie Oliver dish. / *It's my
taste* / you say. / You shuffle through the kitchen / in
open-toed slippers. / Reload the dishwasher / in a *more
efficient* way. / I update you / on the day's events. / 'Boris
is introducing masks in shops / from July the twenty-
fourth'. / Smiling / you say / *The Japanese were right.*

The Day My Husband Buys Me a
Mandarina Duck Rose Dawn Wallet

I can't help but think that the rose leather reeks and that it is insipid compared to my well-worn red and black one. The one I bought with our then four-year-old son, on a trip to the Costa del Sol. The one with a vaccination sticker on, and faded geometric patterns, battered through to the lining. Yes, after all the years that he has not wrapped a present for me, this year, he bought me a wallet. And although my best friend says it's not a big deal, and that it could sit in a drawer, it's strange how much weight you can feel, in an empty wallet. And ironic the brand is Mandarina Duck, and that my sister calls me Mrs. Shoveler because of my pout. And when I thank him and say there was no need since we agreed to have a separate Christmas, I think of all the Burberry wallets given from Japanese husbands to their wives. And when he turns and says he is going to tell me a secret, I feel incredibly awkward. But what he actually says is that he wants me *to carry a comfortable wallet*. That if the money feels comfortable, it will not want to leave a good wallet.

The Japanese Gardener
日本人 の ガーディナー

Since she told him she doesn't love
him, he's taken up gardening,
he's planting her birth flower, a pink rose,
for happiness. He's bought in New Guinea Impatiens –
Busy Lizzies from Home Depot: low maintenance,
guaranteed to flourish. He scrubs and polishes
the decking, for the first time
in their marriage, plants grass with care
to cover arid patches. She watches
through French windows, looking beyond him.

Body Language

You rub up behind me as I wipe the Sainsbury's shop. Like that time babysitting when Bruce, the randy Labrador, stood on his hind legs and whined. I was fourteen and had to shut him outside. He scratched at the door. As I leave for my lockdown walk, you say: *etchi kangaite ne. Etchi*: horny; aroused. Four months ago I took down our wedding photos. That 31-year-old on Waimanolo beach didn't feel like me.

I put up a painting of turbulent waves by Bamburgh fort. The trigger was an argument about Machiko, your sister-in-law. You defended her awfulness to me. Because she is Japanese. And the lack of sex. What do you expect when you've chosen to sleep on a futon in the spare room? And going back to the wedding photos, it took you a month to notice. You said you were so sad you could write a poem.

You say I am no longer *sharp* – a 'loan word' for slim – yet I thought the Japanese love the notion of *shiawase butori*, plump, happily married women. When I lose a few pounds you say: *beijin ne natta ne* – you've regained beauty. Once upon a time, you were all I could see. I watched you sleep.

And the day Scottish Maggie died – lovely mad Maggie, who made me tupperwares of butter tablet – you wouldn't shut up. Kept saying sorry. But you met her only once. I wanted to shout *shut the fuck up*. Sei Sensei says the Japanese are good at carrying boxes when you move house. Today, as I leave this house, you ask, with a teenagerish grin, if I'm having an affair. In the exact same way you ask if I've sorted the recycling.

Unpacking our relationship

LOVE BOMBING

Yamashita Tatsuro's belting out ballads, on the ラジオ, as we head off for Nagano to ski. Your fingers tap tap on my knee. Then, you're serenading me, a Beach Boys cover: *Please Let Me Wonder*, about our future. Tell me to give back my ex his ring. Throw away my wedding album. Phone me in your lunch hour, to say you love *chubby girls*. That you dated an air hostess with *great tits*. You hang a heart around my neck. But are not satisfied. It's smaller than on the Internet.

CIGAR INCIDENT

Remember the day you took me and my black eyes skiing? Lamie said, *things can't be that bad if you two managed to go skiing.* But he wasn't with you as we inched up the mountain. You pushed me to have a cigar the night before. Even though we quit. The cool guy and his wife with colleagues after single malts. And my black eyes? My fault. For not leaving you to sulk. For wanting to talk. But when you're out of sight, Lamie asks if I need to spend a few nights with him and his wife in California.

MIND GAMES

Three times you pretend to throw your wedding ring away. I've fallen from esteemed *sensei* to distance learning student with no income. But you let me binge *Desperate Housewives*, drink Robert Mondavi wine, give me pocket money. And admit how well I click with Gloria & Lamie. It's easier when I'm at business dinners: you needn't speak a lot. And don't I scrub up well, in my black and white polka dots?

BIRTH STORY

You abandon me at Kalamazoo hospital. Not able to perceive how alone I feel in a country where we are strangers. Not able to get that I'm not yet ready to choose a name. When Beatrice picks me up, makes me tea and drives me home, you say you were on the verge of calling the police. You dislike her immensely. Beatrice, who visits me when I give birth, brings homemade tacos to our house. Sees through you, to the real me.

Narcissistic personality disorder

Thirteen years later, in
England, you're Chairman
of the Japanese Golf
Association. You buy
Prosecco, win tournaments.
You write 特別な reports.
Your face is on the web.
Use Re-up hair tonic for
men. Whiten your teeth.
Everyone says you don't
look in your fifties. And
what of my modest poetry
prize? I can donate it to our
domestic account, you tell
our son. You will pay in less
this month.

Gaslighting

When I'm marking essays,
you say it's not appropriate
to be working on a
Saturday. Although you
write *daily reports*, play
Boxing Day golf. You ask
if I've had a diagnosis of
anxiety. Or if it's something
hormonal. You should call
my boss if he's *overloading
me*. But you don't know his
name. On a whim, you take
my computer away. I have
twenty minutes to remove
my work files. Later, you
say you were cleaning it
up. It takes a professional
to tell me, that this is not
acceptable.

Bellinis with Mary

Tucking into Cornish mackerel,
Mary begins to tell me about a friend
who was abused. She left her husband

for an older man. *We all end up
paper thin, don't worry too much
about your other man.* Her friend's man

went to the pool one day and never
came out of the changing room.
I think of bathing costumes. Mum says:

soak the chlorine out. When I returned
from Japan, my swimsuit was lost at Charles de Gaulle.
I wore her tankini to the Roman Baths.

I tell Mary Mum's domineering.
She says, *maybe you married your mother?*
Years of stuff is seeping out:

him leaving me, leaving me
breastfeeding; pretending to throw away
his wedding ring; not speaking.

Another Mary – Mary Jean Chan, has a cycle
for poetry: *rinse & repeat, rinse & repeat.*
But there are some things that can't be washed away.

*

At Gullane Bents

I'm the forty-something working wife,
the one with the *engaging eyes*. I might
have been quite attractive when I was young.
You're sixty-something and colour-blind, need me
to describe the shells on this East Lothian beach.
Stonewashed blue, maybe. The landscape's new
for us, so I borrow your binoculars, scrunching up
one eye, struggling to focus on the perpendicular
dive of a gannet. See oystercatchers,
red-billed, dangling over rocks.

My husband is shooting golf balls
down a well-maintained range. We're here
in the dunes, among the thorny explosion
of sea buckthorn, supposed to hold back erosion.
There are butterflies, gatekeeper and meadow brown.
Gatekeepers have two false eyes
on their wings – *ocelli* – you point them out to me.
Like nectar, this unfamiliar language.
When I cry, a new phrase, in Spanish,
de lágrima fácil: 'of easy tear'.

When I get home, my husband says
he's *glad* I have *come back*. I unpack our shells,
carefully. Wonder why they never
look so good off the beach. Waking up, I think of us.
How you put bicarbonate on your tongue
for morning breath. A home remedy your wife read.
In bed, we listened to Caleb Femi and Seamus Heaney,
seemed to say everything in our heads.

I grab my laptop to record ideas,
placing my finger on the sensor.

But I am caught, off guard,
by the words on my home screen:
this device does not recognise you.

In my King-Size Oak Furnitureland Bed, at 2.27 a.m.

I lie awake, in a night separate
from yours. You sleep on a makeshift bed
with red cushions. I lie on beige pillows, hands thrown
about my head, the way you say makes me look
like a Modigliani model. I think of your white legs,
slight, below your shirt; your selfies,
bold, in the mirror. Since you left her,
you take photos of narcissus petals,
close-up, for me; admire mountain cattle,
how delicately they drink; write cinquains.
I lie here. Wanting you.

When I WhatsApp you in San Lorenzo de El Escorial

I am jealous of the hard-boiled series
you watch from your grotty sofa bed,

and of Sunday morning radio programmes,
which make you laugh. I am jealous

of Harry the hedgehog, tattooed on your arm.
Of the Weird Fish T-shirt that nuzzles

your collarbone. The avocados
that ripen on your radiator.

The hummingbird hawkmoth, hiding
in your sock. I am jealous of

the San Lorenzo bus stop, where you wait
at seven-thirty, an hour ahead of me.

The spreadsheets on your desk.
The well-off students, who get to hear

your silliness, in the messy office
where you eat vegan hummus on spelt bread.

Of *castellana* pots at the entrance to your flat.
Of expats, on terraces eating *patatas bravas*.

I am jealous of the damp patch
in your kitchen. Of your dog, Trasgu.

Yes, I am jealous of Trasgu,
licking your salty feet.

Bickerton's Way

Aberlady, with its Carmelite friary,
stone knight effigy
and algae-heavy ponds,
is where we share New Year
following Postman's Walk
to Bickerton's Way,
trying not to step in dog shit
and wondering if Alice Oswald
got the title for her first collection
from the lovely stone stile
we clamber over.

Long-tailed tits
flit from tree to tree, leaning into
family on shared branches at night time,
you tell me, while we speculate
on their collective noun,
then stop, in muddied boots,
to eat cashews and snog
amidst the yews that have stood
here for centuries. You suggest
a restlessness of tits,
as I tilt my head to watch
through your binoculars.

This tranquil woody scene
reminds me of *The Lady of Shallot*
painting that wallpapers your phone,
and as we near the busy road we turn back
to retreat to Sea Wynd Cottage,

knowing that tomorrow we must
leave for separate homes
and wrestle with the noise.

This is a Confessional Poem
After Kathryn Maris

I am guilty, as I watch you on the screen, of homing
in on your higgledy-piggledy teeth, with gaps
you could park a lorry between. And as you talk
of your Go-Bra-Less, radical feminist daughters,
I think that won't do their boobs any good.
And think of Wendy Pratt's line about jogging –
sweating under each swinging tit, and wonder if I'll keep it up:
'Couch to 5K'. And try as I may, I can't help
but say that their crusade against the patriarchy is undermined
by the fact you pay the rent. After thirty years of teaching,
my dad says: *you can tell a lot from a person's handwriting.*
Mine is *straightforward, honest.*
Sometimes, I am too honest. Like that time
I bumped into my science teacher, Mr. Hull,
on his bicycle, and asked what was wrong
with his legs. He said it was *age, varicose veins.*
And now, looking at you, as you lean
in on WhatsApp, I pretend not to notice the age-gap
but flashback to my school copy of W. H. Auden, his face
looming from the cover, like a tortoise. I tell myself lines
are characterful, dissipate in the evening light. I don't want
to fight. So I try to forget your estranged wife;
your 34-year history. And when you say I'm cruel,
Cruella De Ville and her 101 Dalmatians come to mind,
and I consider how I love a leg of lamb,
but you're vegan, and won't even eat honey.
And I think how, when I'm in my fleece, you say I look
honeybearish. And although this is no teddy bears' picnic,
I crave the handmade-in-Dorset, Belgian chocolate willies,
that lie, stashed away, between my knickers.

Julie Andrews' Honesty

Neither of us is an oil painting, it's true. But
especially true on WhatsApp. With my huge
Italian glasses on, I look like Maureen Lipman
in the British Telecom adverts.
I am not, you say, the woman you met
in person coming smiling down the platform,
in my sunflower dress. But at least
I'm more attractive in the flesh.
Onscreen, you're dripping like a Walls ice cream,
and what with all my wondering what Mum
might make of a *silver-splitter*,
sometimes, I question why we bother. Except
for how hard you make me laugh. When I say
your bum is pert and mine is ample, and you say:
Pert & Ample, like a firm of solicitors.
Or when you dance around your office,
doing the curious moves that only you can do.
And then there's talk of *butlering*
in the noddy, of waking up to
alfresco morning breasts.
And I love the way you notice how I move my head
to emphasize a point, as *only a teacher* can do.
Do it again, you say. And then there's
my *fucking Julie Andrews' Honesty*,
which you've come to love.

Clarty, New Year's Eve 2020

Clarty; I like that word. Bedaubed
with sticky dirt – DIRTY, MUDDY,
STICKY, GOOEY. I click on muddy:
unpure – morally impure. Is that us?
Bedaubed. It's a jewel in my mouth.
Bedaubed. Like debauchery, or baubles,
on a Christmas Tree. I wonder if a pine
feels bedaubed with glittery trinkets.

For weeks now, I have slipped, arse
over tit, on mud and ice. Mud.
I'm caked in it. Fingernails, stuffed.
Laces, rotten. As I trudge this bridleway,
I realise something has happened
in these Gosforth fields – thoughts persist,
stick, become real. And as I take your
New Year's call, whispering your
resolution: the clarty is washed away.

Her

Say you don't think of seeing her in the coffee shop
in Bangor 34 years ago. Say you didn't have nick-
names. Say she didn't love the Shetlands as much
as you do, or drink as much coffee. Say she didn't
sound *disarming* after a glass of wine, and say her
hips weren't *childbearing*, like mine, and that you
didn't tell her you love her as many times a day as
you do me. Say you didn't belly laugh together. And
you didn't write poems dedicated to her. Say you
didn't have an emoji code on WhatsApp. And you've
removed her art, as wallpaper, from your laptop.
Say you didn't turn to her and say *hello darling,
did you sleep okay*? And say she didn't adore your
talk of the notes of the robin in spring, the chime of
great tits. Say she didn't phone you from a mossy log,
with scrunched up beer cans at her feet. Say none of
this, none of this matters. Because *she is not you*.

When I walk with you in El Puerto de Cotos

I want to record how you identify wild boar
by the way they scuff up
the pine floor of the Sierra de Guadarrama.
How you lie, propped on an elbow,
to pluck grassy strands
from a mushroom for a perfect photo.
How you love the little lines around the cap.
Like crimped pie.
To say what we see – mushrooms,
rounded and shiny, like golden manure;
bronze, bell-shaped mushrooms, wearing skirts;
ruddy orange mushrooms, straight from the mouths
of the Brothers Grimm: *falsa oranja*, in Spanish.
To know if all beautiful fungi are poisonous.
To focus my binoculars on the green woodpecker,
its laughing cry and bouncing flight:
3–4 wingbeats, then glide.
To watch clouded yellows duetting
through flora, as we munch peanut butter
between slices of spelt bread. To approach
the large insect striped like a humbug sweet.
To write about coral lichen, draped over
trees, like Halloween frosting,
how delicately it frames the scene.
How now, as I write, I feel
so very far away from the piney Iberian Peninsula.

Writing Guadalupe

You are waiting for my poem about Guadalupe.
Where storks nest in turrets of the Monasterio
de Santa María, where old people sit by the cathedral
and ask what day it is, because time has stopped.

With its coppiced olives and Iberian lynx,
its caramel *torrijas* in the bar of the parador,
where we are lost in cloistered corridors, with saints in alcoves,
paintings of local birds. With its citrus courtyards
where I sing *Oranges and Lemons*.

Valley of the Hidden River,
where I see a greenfinch through binoculars,
its fleck of yellow, that yellow you love.
Where Extremaduran wine flows in a balcony scene
where slightly pissed, I cry. And branches grow.

Guadalupe: pronounced gwah-dah-loo-peh

Snapshots from Beck Hide

Two swans, with grimy plumage.
I ping you the photo. Tell you how
they fought another pair for their
stretch. Do you remember the colony
at Windsor? I told you I preferred
just two, their heads in a heart.

They say a swan can break your arm
defending its territory. I look past
them to a heron, on a post, ignoring
bold young geese congregating in the
duckweed. Canada geese, an invasive
species, *locusts of fresh water.*

Flocks of blue-violet foxgloves.
Yielding digoxin medicine, to tame
your daughter's fluttering heartbeat.
And although she's wary of me, I
understand how grateful you are for
this flower.

And I begin to get her struggle with
me – an invader of her home. Noisily
spitting and hissing, as I watch her,
she unfurls her wings. She's capable
of hurtful blows. But not of serious
damage.

The day you say 'I am not going to spend the rest of my life apologising for my daughter' during our stay near the River Itchen

You clasp your hands behind your head,
spiky, in an Airbnb bed
and I wonder if you'll say the same for me,
refuse to apologise for me:
that woman, that young woman,
that egocentric possessive young woman.
Remember how you translated her words?
Or will it always be this, you shaking your leg,
distracted, when your daughter, your grown-up daughter,
whose had heart troubles since she was three-weeks-old,
gets in your head. I haven't met her yet.
And although she's one-and-a-half-thousand miles away,
when I look at the wild purple foxglove
towering over the other plants in my borders,
I remember how its digoxin protects her heart.
And when you say she'll *come round,*
I think, *I'll never be her mother.*
But back home, on my own, remembering our trip,
I see everything clearly: the sourdough brioche
at the Farmer's market; the guy
who looked like David Jason, who'd given up
London to make Golden Spiced Rum,
who told me to hold it in my mouth *to feel the heat*;
the town guide, Lorraine, who was so much fun,
confusing the deeds of Vikings and Romans,
saying *silly Lorraine!* How hard I dug my nails in
my palm to fight the laughter. And I think of passing
the braided River Itchen: its absolutely pure,

twice-filtered water, running through chalk.
And I recall you telling me there are no others
like it, except the Test. And once again I see us
forging ahead, contemplating the Itchen,
with its one-and-a-half-thousand salmon,
swimming upstream . . .

To G.

after R.F. Langley

Nothing along the road. But poems, maybe. Behind me,
a robin watches from the end of a branch,
as if about to dive. I search for something
to write on. Only my hand. I look up. He's gone. Solitary
berry on tree, I could call it russet, mahogany, perhaps.
Dogs, sniffing about my knees, unafraid. To get close. Wandering
into nettles, brambles. And roe deer, three of them. Starting.
Barking into trees. *Rosa mosqueta*, bright as lipstick, red-peppery,
pressed in my hand. Blackberries, withered and grey. Meandering
the brambled path, pen in one hand, a prickly souvenir in the other:
thistles, teased from scratchy scenery. I could call them fuscous,
dried up. They stick to my coat, I carry a branch
for the hearth. And why do I tell you all this?
Not because I love you or anything. Just, for the giff-gaff.

Don't

stop signing off with two swans
or our virtual pet dog,
Mayakovsky. Don't stop squeaking
kisses through the screen,
showing the whites of your eyeballs.
Don't stop delighting me
with pictures of bladderwrack
and blackcap. Inventing
words like *indeediedoodums*.
Saying *do you know how much
I love you*: arms and legs splayed
from your Spanish bed. Don't stop
meeting me on the platform
in a Conductor's hat. Kissing me
in a cloistered abbey housing
Catherine of Aragon. Saying
I'm looking *very Anna Karenina*,
in my fluffy dressing gown.
Adding it's not a good analogy
since she threw herself
in front of a train. Having naked tea,
propped up by Holiday Inn pillows.
Sending me billowing Malaga
biznaga, whose scent makes me
dizzy. And although I'm
a little bit wobbly, and your big toes
curl in different directions,
let's keep stepping out.

Home

I want a place
where when I say the words
I'm home, I alter your state of mind.
A place where you raise an eyebrow
when I bite my nails.
A place where we savour
vanilla coffee from a cafetière.
Where when you wear
your Conductor's hat
(supposed to be *Adult
Deluxe* but comes up small)
we fall about with laughter.
Where jokes yoke us.
A place where we crack each other open.
Where, when I'm tinkering
with a poem, you slip
your arm around my waist.
And I interrupt you, lost
in Kafka's *Castle*.
A place where we care enough
to ask after each other's
parents. Where we no longer
suffer *skin hunger*. A place
where boundaries, boundaries
of us, begin to blur: charcoal
gently rubbed into a page,
the composition of you and me
has soft edges.

The day I tell you I had no knickers on
when the Sainsbury's man called

we laugh, and I want more of this.
I want more of kicking up
my peep-toe heels, holding hands
in fields, as elderly scouts
go by with rambling staffs
and appreciative looks. I want more
of your bookishness. Your love
of Almodóvar scripts:
you can't smell or taste success!
More of you calling me sybaritic
on observing my *tipsy truffle*
habit. Of sharing peaty Laphroig
from a sporran flask engraved
with the words: *What larks, G!*
Miss Haversham on your crappy TV
your feet up, in kingfisher socks.
You pet naming me, my Beautiful Birder,
as we let others pass, on Aberlady Bridge,
and spot a Little stomping Egret
on clumsy yellow feet.
More of pterodactyl cormorants
seen from the hide where you get me
to say *murciélago!* Bats, in Spanish.
And more of exploring
the East Lothian coast, of getting lost
in the dunes of Gullane Bents
among marshland snipe
and disused tank defences.
Yes, I want more of us.

Unbridled

I'm thinking of Andrea McLean – I
cried when she left *Loose Women*,
how openly she spoke of loneliness

in a marriage. My thoughts turn to
our beach wedding: you and me, and
an expenses spreadsheet. We wore

Hawaiian leis. Auntie Anne said it
was like 'An Officer and a Gentle-
man'. I remember you covered my
mouth when I came.

I'm in a poetry workshop with Jack
Underwood: patterns in language –
the tyranny of the habitual, how dull
it can be, our tendency to talk of a
line of trees. I think of the quote

from Gibran about the cypress and
the oak, failing to grow in each
other's shadow; and of the scold's
bridle to tame women. Since I told

you I don't love you anymore, you've
taken up gardening. My birth flower
is a pink rose – for happiness.

I'm on the phone to Dad before
Corrie.

He says the affair between Alina and
Tyrone is ridiculous – I say, 'I'll give
you get back to your *Corrie*'. And
wonder why you encouraged me to
debate at Oxford, but not to speak up

about day-to-day stuff. I recall you
say: *he's from a different culture.* You
remind me of what Granny Corrin

said: *don't shit in your own nest.* And
I think of the witch's bridle – a cage
for the head – to silence women.

But then there's you, G. – our
WhatsApp routine – the joking about
my Couch to 5K, on the bridleway.
You're imagining runaway brides in
wedding gowns and I'm telling you
how freely the horses stomp about.
Unrestrained, uncontainable.

And I think of TV's Miranda, how
she says women should make gallop-
ing a thing, should gallop

through shopping malls. I picture her.
Galloping along for all she's worth.
Mouth hanging open –

Sing Me Down from the Dark

In the thickets of San Lorenzo Park, you've finally found your nightingale. The nightingale, rich in song, but mousy in colour. Dull. Something I'll never call you. When we met on Zoom, you hid behind a Moroccan mask. Because you're all about the daft. *Yes,* you said, *my wife is Spanish.* There's 1,600 km between us. A fraction of the 4,800 km the nightingale flies from West Africa. The boy nightingale serenades the migrating girls, from the thorny dark. *It's just astonishing,* you say. *How they out-sing the skylark. Do you think it's a conscious thing, to shake up their repertoire?* I consider whether it deliberately changes its tune. We talk of me and you, of growing into each other, of gathering mutual points of reference, of a long East Lothian weekend, with a local malt. And I think of how once these nightingales, caged for their song, would kill themselves dashing against their rails, trying to fulfil their migratory urge.

Acknowledgements

With thanks to the following journals in which some of these poems first appeared: *Anthropocene, Artemis, Diamond Twig, Fenland Poetry Journal, London Grip, Obsessed with Pipework, Orbis, Poetry Wales, Porridge, Silver Needle Press* (USA), *Snakeskin, SPELT, Streetlight Magazine* (USA), *Tears in the Fence, The Alchemy Spoon, The Cannon's Mouth, The Frogmore Papers, The High Window, The Moth, The North* and *The Ofi Press*. Thanks also to the editors of the following anthologies: *un-seaming the tendon* (Winning poems from the 2020 Winchester Poetry Prize), *so we go about our days* (Winchester Poetry Prize 2021) and the 2021 *Live Canon Anthology*.

Sincere appreciation to Oxford Brookes International Poetry competition for awarding 'Wakeboarding in Hamamatsu' a special commendation in the 2020 Open competition. 'At the Fishmonger's with my Son', 'This is a Confessional Poem', 'At Gullane Bents' and 'The Day My Husband Buys Me a Mandarina Duck Rose Dawn Wallet' were shortlisted by Billy Collins for the Fish prize in 2020, 2021 and 2022. 'Bride Face', was shortlisted for the same prize, by Ellen Bass, in 2018. 'When I WhatsApp you in San Lorenzo de El Escorial' was shortlisted for the 2021 Troubadour prize.

I would also like to thank the people involved, one way or another, in propelling this collection forward. First, love and thanks to my mentor, Heidi Williamson, who gave me exactly the tools I needed to develop my writing, taught me to write what's in my head, and to take tremendous joy in the process. Huge thanks as well to my powerhouse Poetry School tutors, Tamar Yoseloff and Jacqueline Saphra, who I count myself supremely lucky to have met. Thanks, in equal measure, to my friend and supporter, David Caddy, who I have loved having in my corner!

Thanks also to the following individuals, whose words of encouragement and practical support are deeply appreciated: Helena Nelson, Nial Munro, Zoë Brigley, Fiona Benson, Andrew McMillan, George Simmers, Sue Burge, Anna Woodford, Pippa Little and Elisabeth Sennitt Clough. I also wish to express my gratitude to the following groups: The Canada Water Group, Read and Respond, and Creative Constraints, and to my dear friends, Natalie Crick and Rebecca Bailey, for sharing in my enthusiasms and obsessions, and to Rebecca particularly, for proof-reading the manuscript.

Sing me down from the dark would not exist if Christopher Hamilton-Emery and Jennifer Hamilton-Emery had not seen me perform on a stage in March, in the Fenlands. I cannot thank them enough for believing in me and for making this happen. And for Christopher's enviable efficiency and patience with my excruciating edits! Finally, love and thanks to Mum and Dad, for sending me to Speech and Drama lessons with Mrs. Buthlay, for getting me hooked on poetry, and for their excitement about the collection, which means everything.